MY BODY

by Patricia Carratello

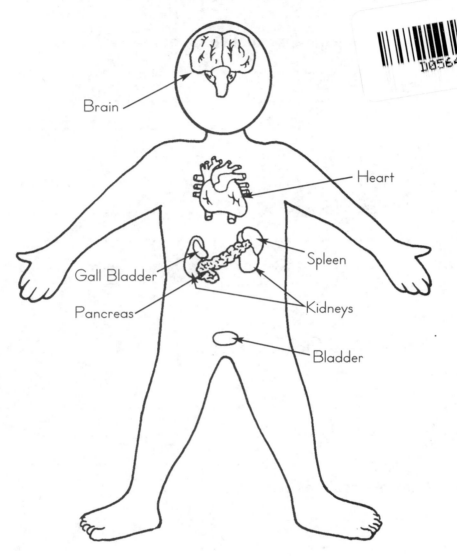

Brain

Heart

Gall Bladder

Pancreas

Spleen

Kidneys

Bladder

Teacher Created Resources, Inc.
6421 Industry Way
Westminster, CA 92683
www.teachercreated.com
ISBN: 978-1-55734-211-9

©1980 Teacher Created Resources, Inc.
Reprinted, 2010
Made in U.S.A.

Table of Contents

Introduction 3
Body Pattern #1 4
Body Pattern #1 (Includes Reproductive Organs) 5
Body Pattern #2 6
My Brain. 7
My Heart. 9
My Kidneys 11
My Bladder 11
My Kidneys and My Bladder 12
My Cells 13
My Spleen 13
My Pancreas 14
My Gall Bladder 14
My Pancreas, Spleen, and Gall Bladder 15
My Reproductive Organs 17
My Skeleton 19
My Muscles 22
My Stomach. 25
My Small and Large Intestines 27
My Small Intestine. 28
My Large Intestine 29
My Liver 30
My Lungs 32
My Skin. 35
My Eyes 36
My Nose 36
My Ears 37
My Tongue 37
My Face 38
My Body Checklist 39

Introduction

This book is designed to provide information about the human body for the primary child. The teacher may copy its pages for use with students.

Parts of the human body are explained and illustrated. There are several ways that these explanations and illustrations can be used.

1. Make a full-size tracing of each child's body on tagboard or other sturdy paper.

2. Cut, paste, color, and follow directions to make the various parts of the body.

3. Look at the "body patterns" and place the body parts correctly on the traced body.

4. Copy the explanations of the functions of the body parts. Discuss the information with the students.

5. Make the explanation sheets into a book and fasten with brads or yarn. (Children learning writing skills can copy these explanations off the board as a writing exercise.)

6. Have each child take the booklet home along with his or her completed "life-size" body. It will be fun to share with the family!

It is our hope that if children learn about their bodies at an early age, they will not abuse them later. We hope they will join with us and become excited about learning what is going on inside the body and strive to stay healthy!

Body Pattern #1

• Use as body-part layout guide. Paste all parts directly on paper body, except bladder.

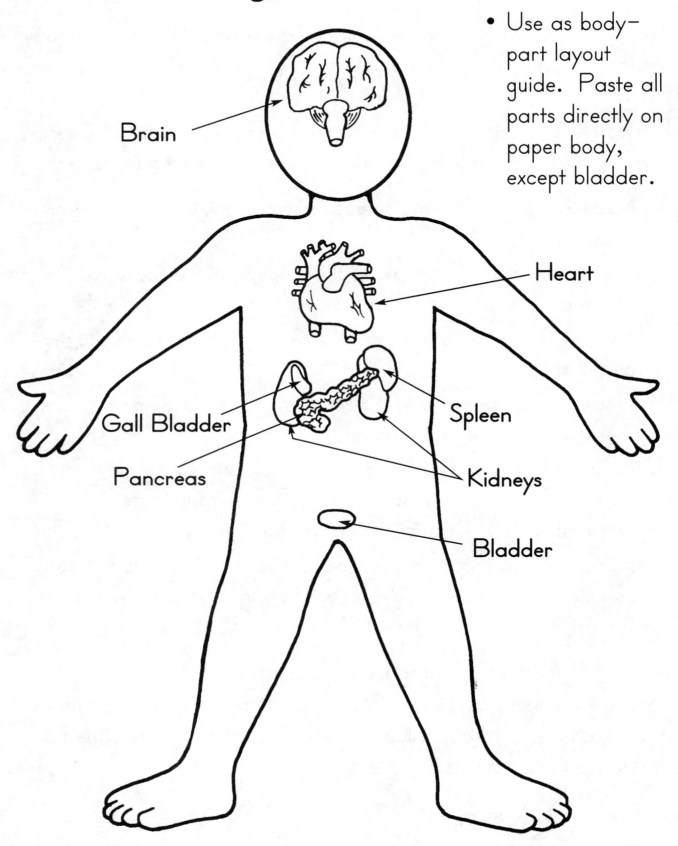

Brain

Heart

Gall Bladder

Spleen

Pancreas

Kidneys

Bladder

Body Pattern #1
(Includes Reproductive Organs)

- Use as body-part layout guide. Paste all parts directly on paper body, except bladder.

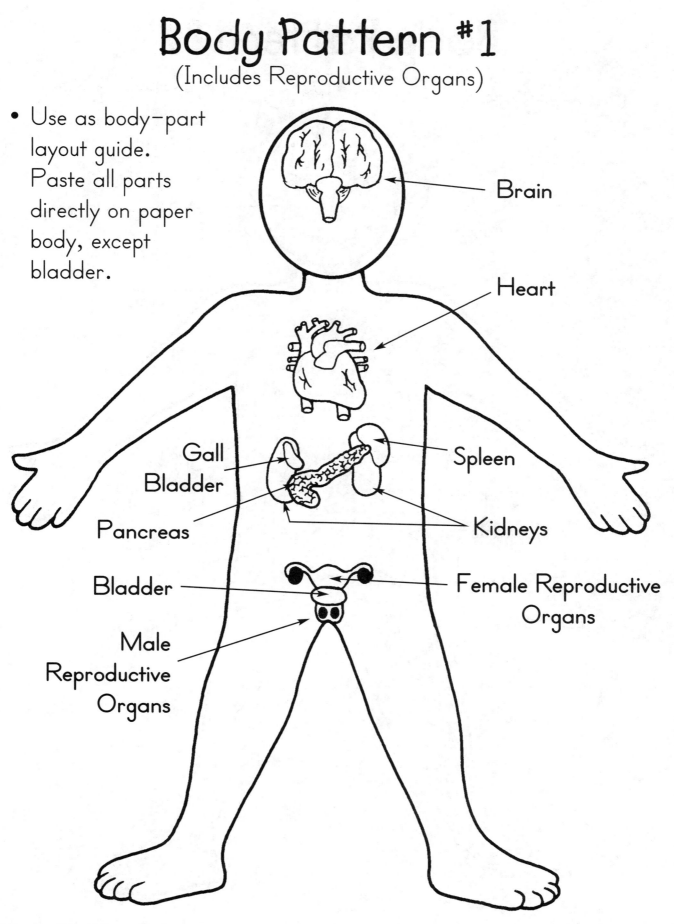

Brain

Heart

Gall Bladder

Spleen

Pancreas

Kidneys

Bladder

Female Reproductive Organs

Male Reproductive Organs

Body Pattern #2

• Use after Body Pattern #1 is completed.

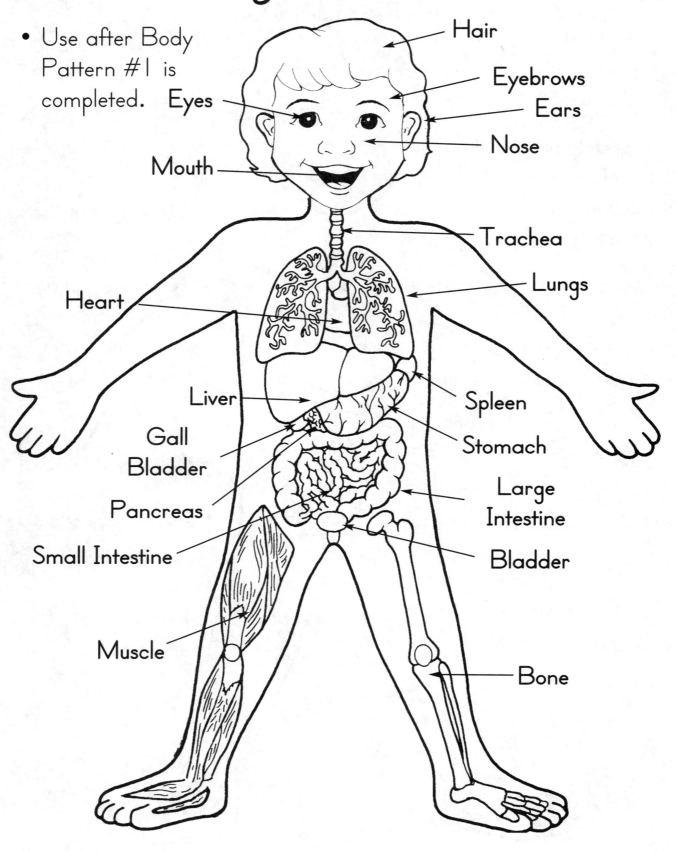

Hair

Eyebrows

Ears

Nose

Eyes

Mouth

Trachea

Lungs

Heart

Liver

Spleen

Stomach

Gall Bladder

Pancreas

Large Intestine

Small Intestine

Bladder

Muscle

Bone

My Brain

My brain works hard. It is like a computer that answers my questions and sends messages all over my body.

My brain looks wrinkled, like a walnut shell. It will weigh between two and three pounds when I am an adult. My brain is very fragile and soft. It needs to be protected. My brain is protected by a very hard bone called my skull. If I touch the top of my head, I can feel my skull. My brain is inside my skull!

I have many nerves in my brain. My nerves are like little telephone lines that send messages all over my body. Most of these messages go to my body through my spinal cord. Messages from my brain move very quickly through my body. They move faster than I can blink my eyes!

My brain keeps my heart beating and my lungs breathing. It makes me move. My brain makes me think and helps me remember things.

My brain helps me talk, write, see, smell, hear, and many other things. It even helps keep me from falling down!

My brain works hard for me.

My Brain *(cont.)*

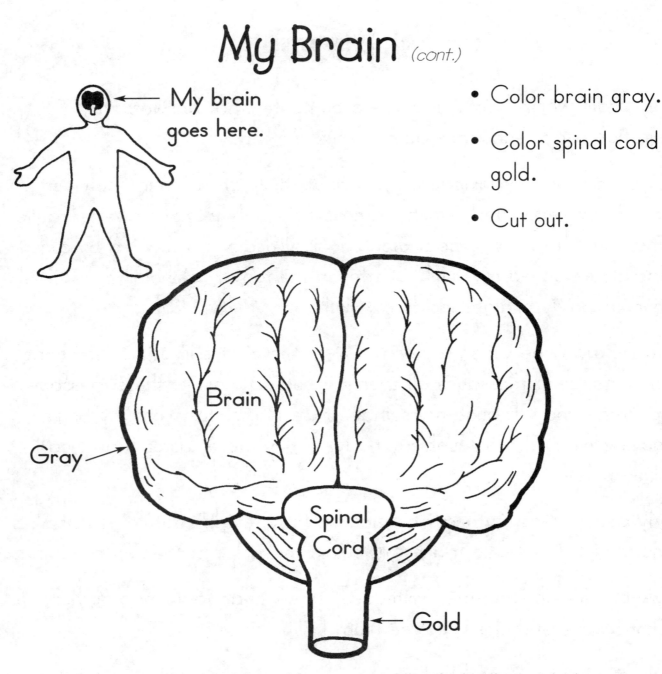

My brain goes here.

- Color brain gray.

- Color spinal cord gold.

- Cut out.

Gray

Brain

Spinal Cord

Gold

- Paste on top part of head as in diagram. (Leave a little room for some hair!)

- When the face is pasted on, the eyes are even with the top part of the spinal cord. Do not paste the face on the brain. Paste the nose, mouth, and chin area. You will still be able to pull away the top of the face and see the brain!

- The face fits exactly over the brain.

My Heart

My heart is a strong pump that moves blood through my body. It hangs in the center of my chest and is about the size of my fist.

My heart works all the time, even when I am sleeping. It pumps blood that is full of oxygen and food through tubes called arteries. This fresh blood travels to all my cells and feeds them. My blood also cleans my cells. My cells give the blood carbon dioxide and other things they can't use. Then, my blood moves back to the heart through tubes called veins.

My heart pumps this used blood to my lungs. My lungs take out the carbon dioxide and put in new, fresh oxygen. Then, my blood goes back to my heart to work again.

It takes about one minute for my heart to circle blood around my body and back again. This is called circulation.

I can hear my heart working all the time. The beating sound my heart makes is caused by the opening and closing of the valves inside my heart. These valves are like doors. They let the blood in and out of my heart.

So when I hear or feel my heart beating, I know my blood is circling all around my body. My heart moves the blood to clean and feed my cells.

My Heart *(cont.)*

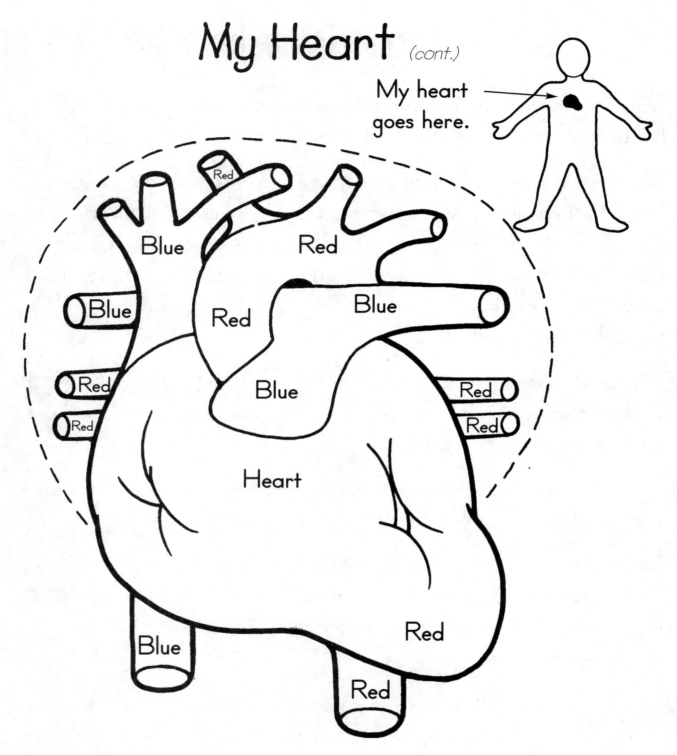

My heart goes here.

Blue

Red

Blue

Red

Blue

Red

Red

Blue

Red

Blue

Red

Heart

Red

Blue

Red

- Color heart red and blue. Arteries (red) carry oxygen. Veins (blue) carry carbon dioxide.

- Cut out (on solid or broken lines).

- Put heart on your paper body with paste.

My Kidneys

I have two kidneys. My kidneys are wonderful filters for my body. They help make my blood pure.

My blood passes through my two kidneys after it has fed and cleaned my cells. My kidneys separate any liquid waste from my blood. Then, my kidneys send the liquid waste my body can't use down to my bladder. My kidneys send any liquid that can still be used back to my blood.

My kidneys keep my blood clean!

My Bladder

My bladder is a storehouse for liquid waste.

When my kidneys have cleaned my blood, they send all the liquid waste to my bladder. All this waste, or urine, is stored until the bladder becomes full. When my bladder is full of urine, my brain sends a signal that tells me it is time to empty it!

My Kidneys and My Bladder

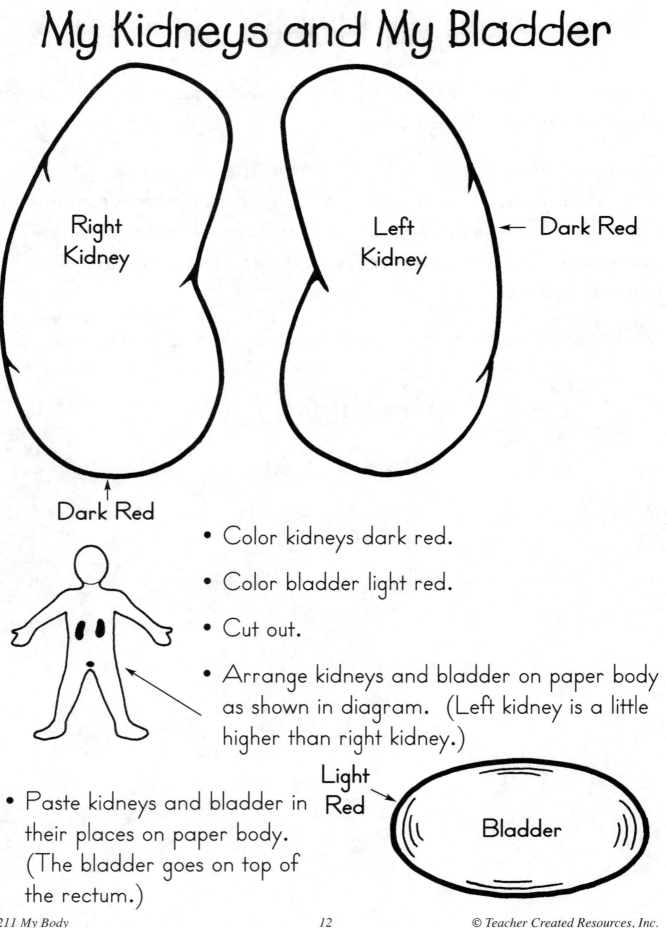

Right
Kidney

Left
Kidney

← Dark Red

↑
Dark Red

- Color kidneys dark red.

- Color bladder light red.

- Cut out.

- Arrange kidneys and bladder on paper body as shown in diagram. (Left kidney is a little higher than right kidney.)

- Paste kidneys and bladder in their places on paper body. (The bladder goes on top of the rectum.)

Light
Red

Bladder

My Cells

The cell is the start of all life. Every part of me is made up of one or more tiny things called cells.

My cells are different shapes and sizes. They grow into the shapes and sizes my body needs. Some of my cells are needed to make my muscles. Some are needed to make my blood. And some of my cells are needed for my skin, especially if I fall down and cut myself! My skin can grow back with these new cells!

My body makes over a billion new cells every minute! My cells grow and divide all my life. They need food and oxygen to help them grow. My blood takes my cells the food and oxygen they need. My blood gets these things from the food I eat and the air I breathe.

My Spleen

My spleen works for my blood. It helps destroy worn-out red blood cells. My spleen sends any leftover usable cell parts back to be reused in the making of new red blood cells. My spleen also stores some red blood cells. It gives these red blood cells to my body when I need them.

My spleen also helps make white blood cells. These white blood cells are fighters that help destroy infections in my body.

My Pancreas

My pancreas is a gland that helps me digest my food. It is also very important in my body's use of sugar.

My pancreas makes a liquid called pancreatic juice. This juice is sent to my small intestine. It helps break my food apart so my body can use it.

My pancreas also makes a very important substance called insulin. Insulin helps my body burn the food sugars I eat. This burning of my food sugar makes heat and energy that my body needs and uses.

My Gall Bladder

My gall bladder is a storehouse for my body. It is under my liver and is shaped like a pear.

My gall bladder stores a greenish–yellowish liquid called bile. Bile is made by my liver. Bile helps my body break down and use fats. Bile also helps make stomach acid harmless.

My gall bladder is a storehouse for bile in my body.

My Pancreas, Spleen, and Gall Bladder

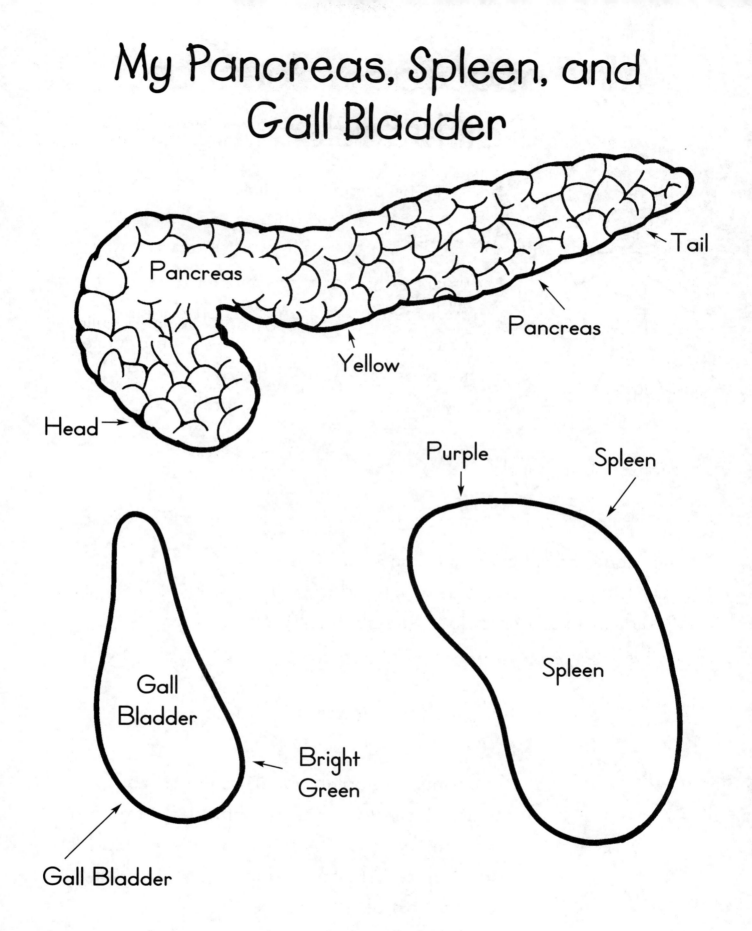

Pancreas

Tail

Pancreas

Yellow

Head

Purple

Spleen

Gall Bladder

Bright Green

Spleen

Gall Bladder

My Pancreas, Spleen, and Gall Bladder (cont.)

- Color the pancreas yellow.

- Cut out.

- Arrange the pancreas as in diagram. Paste middle section of pancreas on paper body. (The "head" and the "tail" of the pancreas should be free so that they can be lifted to show the kidneys underneath.)

- Color spleen purple.

- Cut out.

- Arrange the spleen as in diagram. Paste spleen along upper edges of left kidney. (You should still be able to see about half of the kidney.)

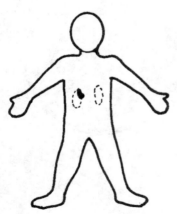

- Color gall bladder bright green.
- Cut out.
- Arrange the gall bladder as in diagram. Paste top part of the gall bladder on top part of right kidney. (Bottom part of gall bladder will flap over large intestine. The liver will cover most of gall bladder.)

My Reproductive Organs

I have organs inside my body that I can't see. One day these organs will make it possible for me to be a mother or a father. These organs are called my reproductive organs.

If I am a girl, I have the female reproductive organs. These parts will become more developed as I get older. I have two ovaries. My two ovaries contain eggs. I have a uterus. My uterus can be a home for a baby to grow in before it is born.

If I am a boy, I have the male reproductive organs. These parts will become more developed as I get older. I have two testicles. My two testicles will make sperm.

One day, these organs may make it possible to be a mother or a father!

My Reproductive Organs *(cont.)*

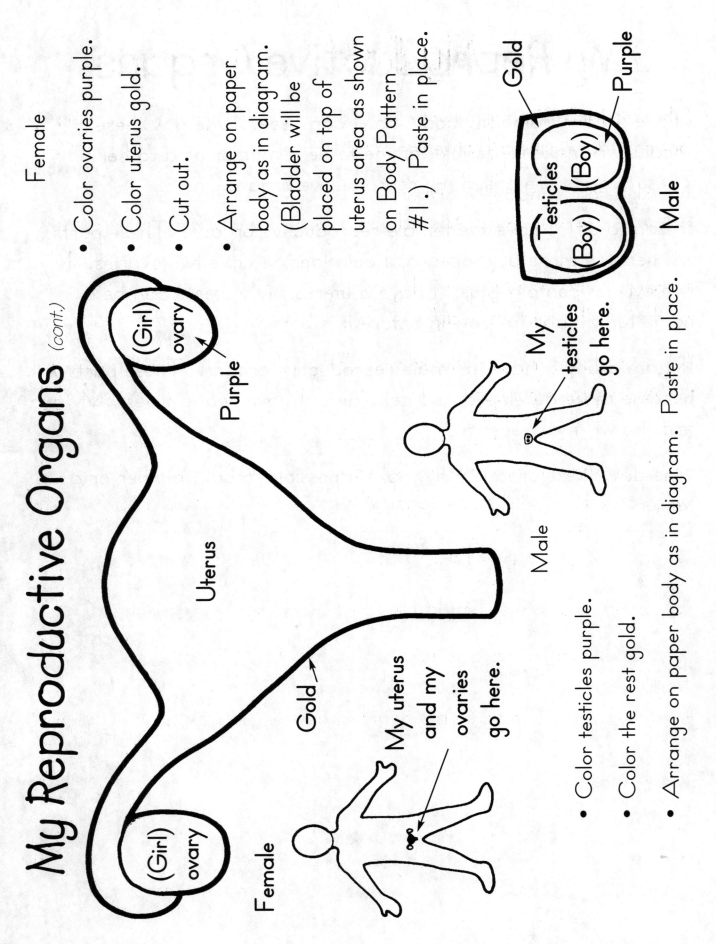

Female

- Color ovaries purple.
- Color uterus gold.
- Cut out.
- Arrange on paper body as in diagram. (Bladder will be placed on top of uterus area as shown on Body Pattern #1.) Paste in place.

(Girl) ovary — Purple

Uterus — Gold

(Girl) ovary

Female

My uterus and my ovaries go here.

Testicles (Boy) — Gold

(Boy) — Purple

Male

My testicles go here.

Male

- Color testicles purple.
- Color the rest gold.
- Arrange on paper body as in diagram. Paste in place.

My Skeleton

My skeleton is the framework for all my body. It is like the strong boards that make a framework for a house.

My skeleton is made up of bones. My bones are hard and they do not weigh very much. When I was a baby, my bones were soft. Now, as I am getting older, my bones are getting harder and harder. My bones grow as I grow. I have 206 bones, and many of them will grow this year!

My bones give my body its shape. If I did not have my bones, I would bend like rubber!

My bones are joined together at places called joints. My joints are made strong by tough tissues called ligaments. My joints are lined with something called cartilage. My cartilage acts like a pad that keeps my bones from crashing into each other. My joints let me move my bones. (My knee lets my leg bend!)

My body also makes brand new cells inside some of my bones.

My bones protect organs inside my body, too. My skull protects my fragile, soft brain. If I touch my chest, I can feel my ribs. My ribs are the bones that cover my heart and lungs and protect them.

My skeleton does many things for me.

My Skeleton (cont.)
My Bones

My bones go here.

- Reproduce on white or off-white (ivory) paper.

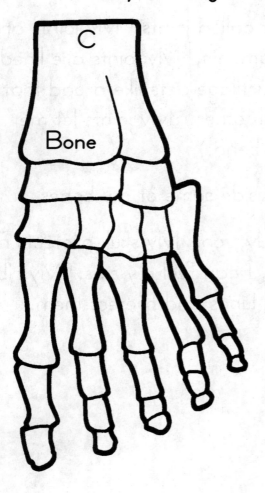

- Cut out bones of the leg. Arrange the bones of the leg inside the left leg. (Big toe should be on the inside as in diagram.)

- Paste on leg. The foot joins at "C." The two kneecaps are "combined." (Paste kneecap "A" over kneecap "B.")

My
Skeleton _(cont.)_

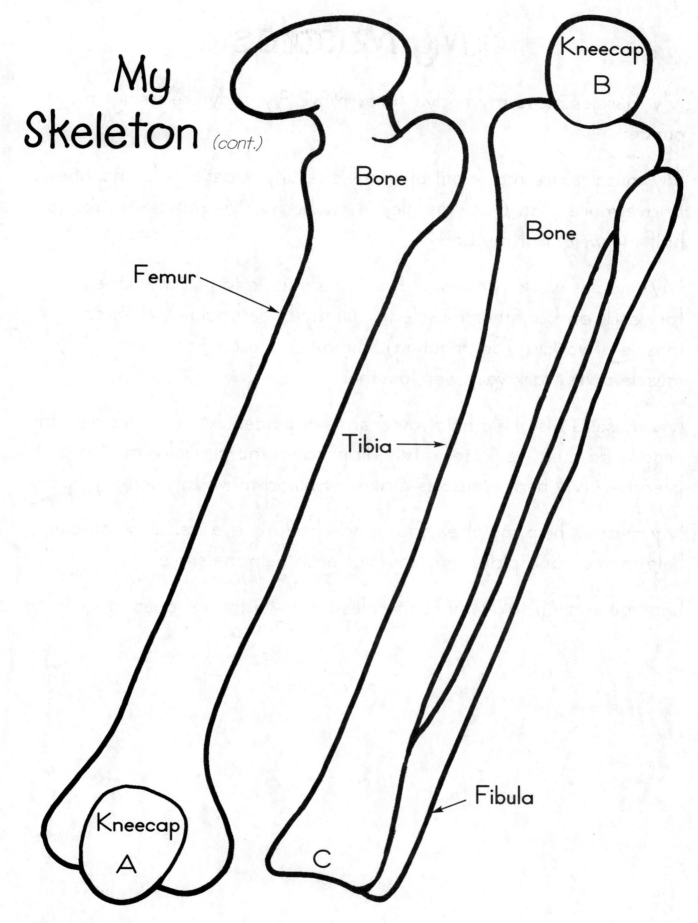

Kneecap B

Bone

Bone

Femur

Tibia

Fibula

Kneecap A

C

My Muscles

My muscles move my body. They move my body like strings move a puppet!

My muscles are made out of many stretchy, elastic cells and fibers. I have more than 600 muscles in my body. My muscles make up half the weight of my body!

My muscles work in pairs. I have one muscle to pull my bone forward, and another muscle to pull my bone back. When one muscle is working (contracting), the other muscle is relaxing. My muscle pairs work very well together.

My muscles also help hold my organs in place. My muscles help my organs do their work, too. My diaphragm muscle helps my lungs breathe. My heart muscles make my blood move through my body.

My muscles help me chew food and close my eyelids. My muscles help me run and play. My muscles even help me smile!

Did you know it takes more muscles to frown than it does to smile?

My Muscles *(cont.)*

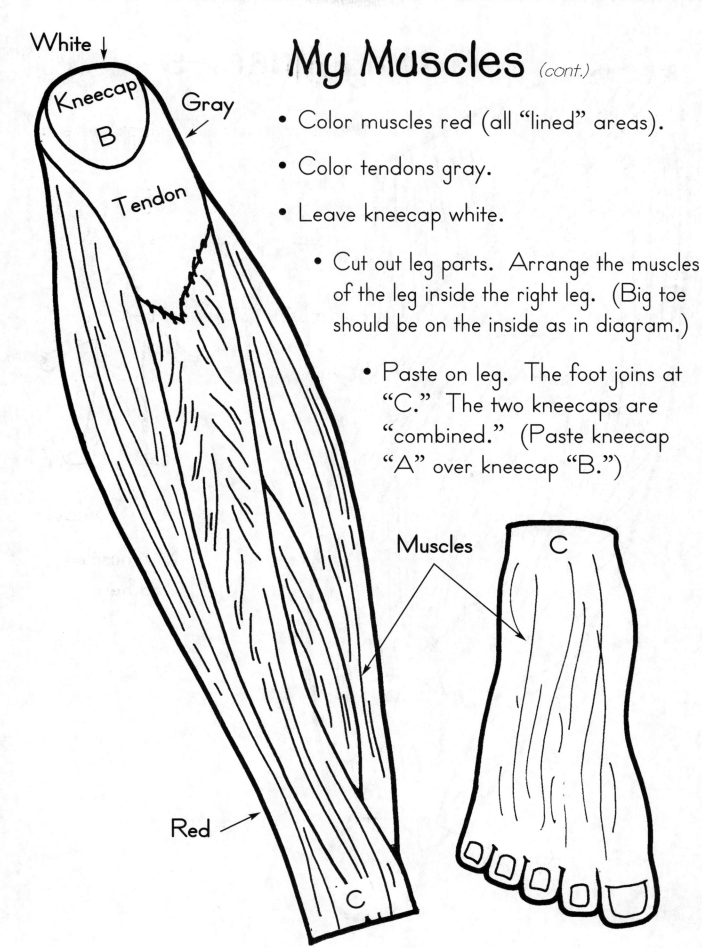

- Color muscles red (all "lined" areas).

- Color tendons gray.

- Leave kneecap white.

- Cut out leg parts. Arrange the muscles of the leg inside the right leg. (Big toe should be on the inside as in diagram.)

- Paste on leg. The foot joins at "C." The two kneecaps are "combined." (Paste kneecap "A" over kneecap "B.")

White ↓

Kneecap

B

Gray

Tendon

Muscles

C

Red

C

My Muscles (cont.)

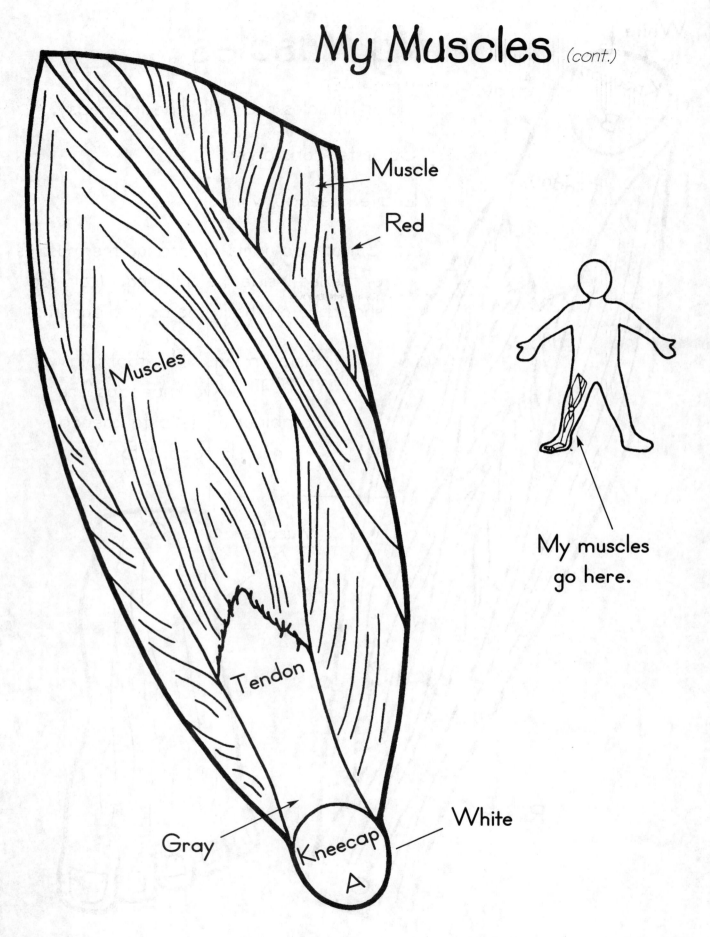

Muscle

Red

Muscles

Tendon

Gray

Kneecap
A

White

My muscles
go here.

My Stomach

My stomach is like a stretchy bag that holds my food after I eat. My stomach also helps to break my food into smaller pieces so my body can use it.

About 10 seconds after I swallow my food, it reaches my stomach. My food reaches my stomach through a tube called my esophagus. Little glands in my stomach make special juices that are waiting for my food. Once my food enters my stomach, my muscles move the walls of my stomach. My stomach mashes my food the way a baker kneads dough for bread! My food gets mashed and stirred with the special juices. The juices and the mashing help to break my food into smaller pieces, or "digest" it.

My stomach has a door in it that closes to keep food inside. My stomach keeps food inside to work on for a few hours. My stomach can stretch out to hold almost two quarts of food!

When my stomach has digested my food as much as it can, the door opens and my food travels into my small intestine.

When my stomach is empty, it shrinks like a balloon without air!

My stomach is a stretchy storage tank!

My Stomach *(cont.)*

- Color stomach orange.

- Cut out.

- Position stomach as in diagram. (Esophagus tube will be under heart. Stomach will be over left kidney and partly covering spleen and pancreas.)

- Make sure that stomach attaches to the small intestine at the lower tube.

- Attach stomach with brad at dot.

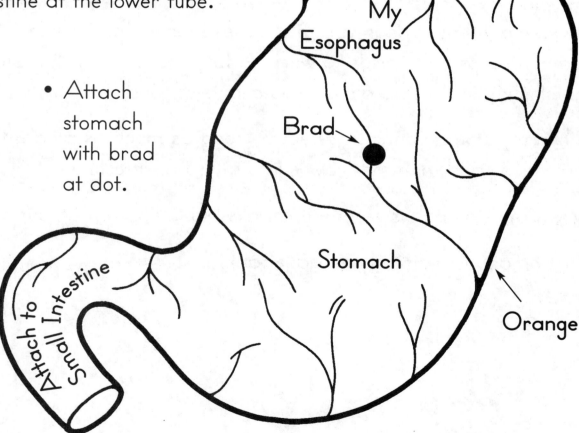

To My Esophagus

Brad

Stomach

Orange

Attach to Small Intestine

My Small and Large Intestines

My small intestine is about 20 feet long. My food is pushed slowly through the twists and turns of my small intestine. The muscle wall of my small intestine does the pushing.

My food is digested as it is pushed through my small intestine. Digestive enzymes break my food into tiny, tiny parts. My body keeps my food in my small intestine until it is digested well. The digestion takes from four to eight hours.

After my food is digested, it is ready to go into my blood and work for my body. My food is stopped in my small intestine by tiny, hairy, finger-like things called villi. My villi suck in (absorb) all the usable food and give it to my blood. Then, the villi help to pass the waste down to my large intestine.

My large intestine gets the waste products from my small intestine. The waste stays in my large intestine for 10 to 12 hours.

The waste is pushed through my five feet of large intestine by the muscle wall. Some water from the waste is taken out. Then, the solid waste is pushed out of my body through the rectum.

It takes about 24 hours for my food to travel from my mouth to my rectum!

My Small Intestine

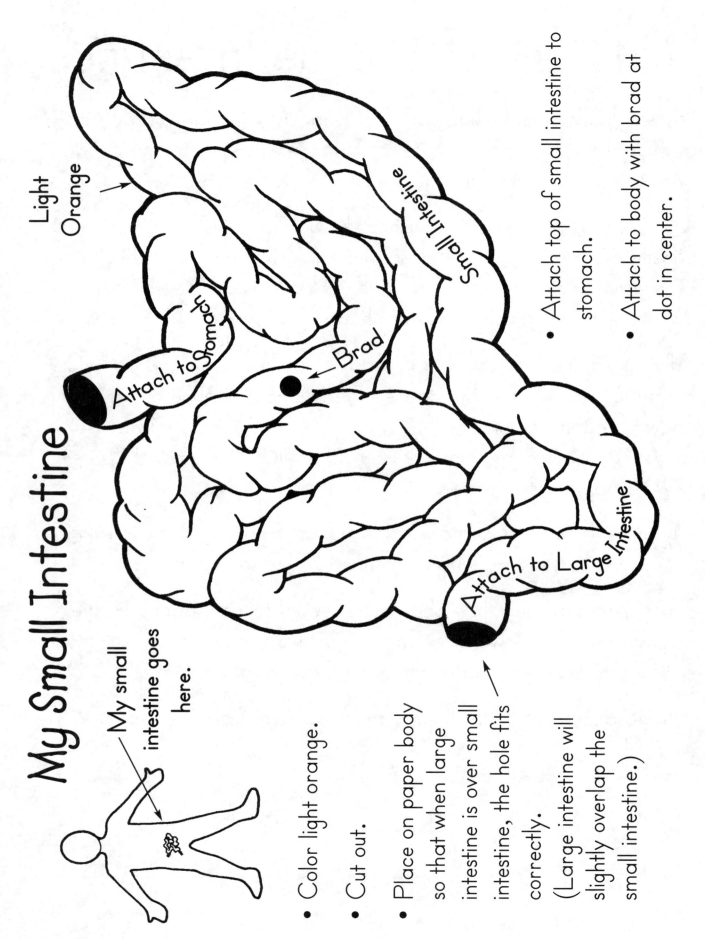

Light Orange

Small Intestine

Attach to Stomach

Brad

Attach to Large Intestine

- Attach top of small intestine to stomach.
- Attach to body with brad at dot in center.

My small intestine goes here.

- Color light orange.
- Cut out.
- Place on paper body so that when large intestine is over small intestine, the hole fits correctly. (Large intestine will slightly overlap the small intestine.)

28

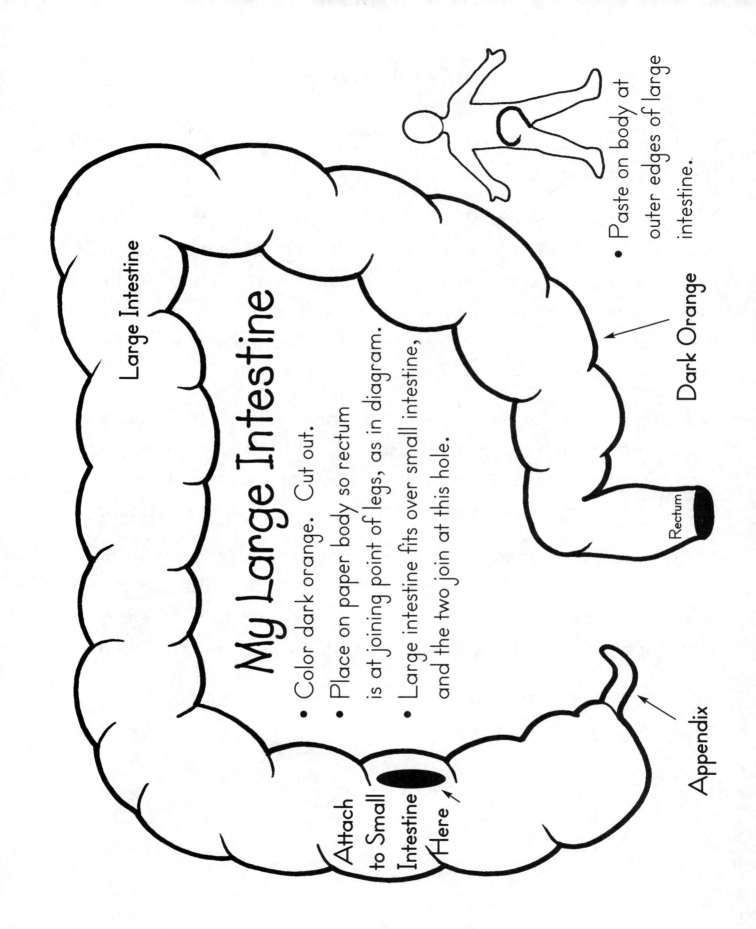

Large Intestine

My Large Intestine

- Color dark orange. Cut out.
- Place on paper body so rectum is at joining point of legs, as in diagram.
- Large intestine fits over small intestine, and the two join at this hole.

Rectum

- Paste on body at outer edges of large intestine.

Dark Orange

Appendix

Attach to Small Intestine Here

My Liver

My liver helps my body do many things. My liver is a very important factory and storehouse for my body.

My liver helps clean my blood. My liver works hard to clean the blood that is used to digest my food. My liver takes out worn-out red blood cells. It also fights and destroys things in my blood that might poison my body. Then my liver sends all the waste products it has cleaned out of my blood down to my intestines. From there, they are sent out of my body.

My liver takes things out of my blood that are good for my body, too! My liver takes out vitamins, sugars, and other usable parts of food. My liver stores many of these food parts until my body needs them. Then, my liver sends them to my body through my blood.

My liver can also make things. It can make new liver cells when the old ones are worn out or damaged. My liver can make disease fighters called antibodies. My liver can also make bile. Bile is a very important liquid that helps me digest the food I eat so I can use it.

My liver is a very important factory and storehouse in my body.

My Liver (cont.)

Reddish-Brown

Liver

Brad

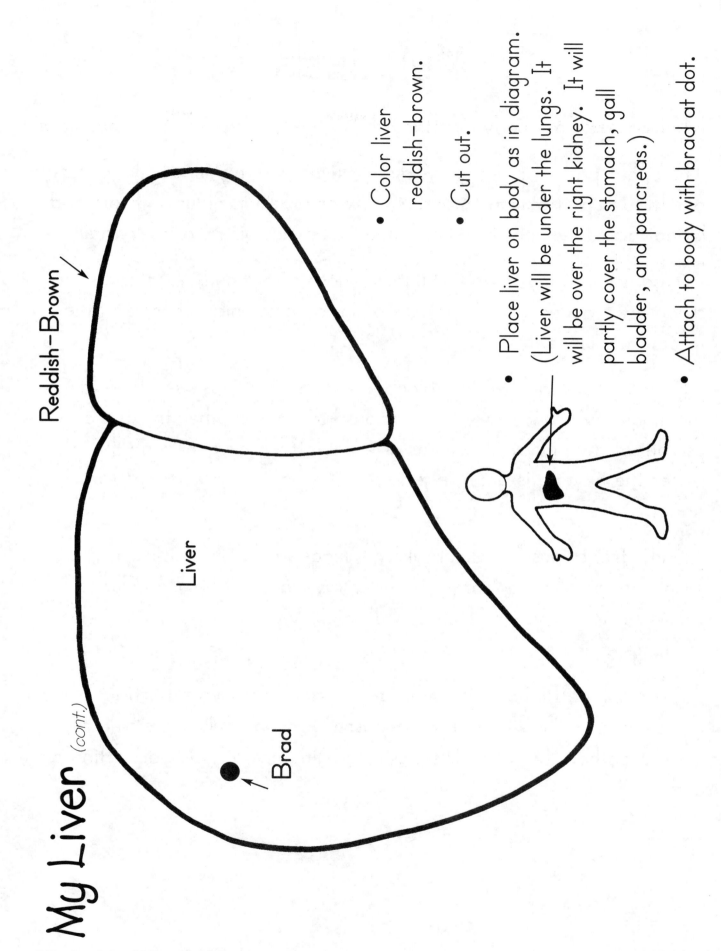

- Color liver reddish-brown.

- Cut out.

- Place liver on body as in diagram. (Liver will be under the lungs. It will be over the right kidney. It will partly cover the stomach, gall bladder, and pancreas.)

- Attach to body with brad at dot.

My Lungs

My lungs help my body breathe.

The upper part of my chest is almost filled with my lungs. My lungs are made up of millions of elastic-like sacs which fill up with air and let out air. My lungs can hold about as much air as a basketball!

Air comes into my body through my nose and mouth. It travels down my trachea (windpipe), through my bronchial tubes, and then to both my lungs.

My lungs trade air with my blood. My heart pumps used blood to my lungs. My lungs take the carbon dioxide and other things I can't use out of my blood. My lungs give back fresh oxygen to my blood. After the trading is done, my blood goes back to my heart to work again.

A big, strong muscle helps make my lungs work. It is called my diaphragm. My diaphragm is under my lungs. It helps my lungs expand when they are filling up with air. My diaphragm also helps my lungs squeeze out the used air.

So, every time I inhale (breathe air in) and every time I exhale (breathe air out), I know my lungs are working. My lungs help my body breathe. They are like balloons filling up with air and letting air out!

My Lungs *(cont.)*

- Color lungs pink and airway light blue.

- Cut out both lungs.

- Paste trachea A on top of trachea B. Now there is just one trachea.

- Paste trachea on paper body, starting at chin as in the diagram. Paste entire trachea on body.

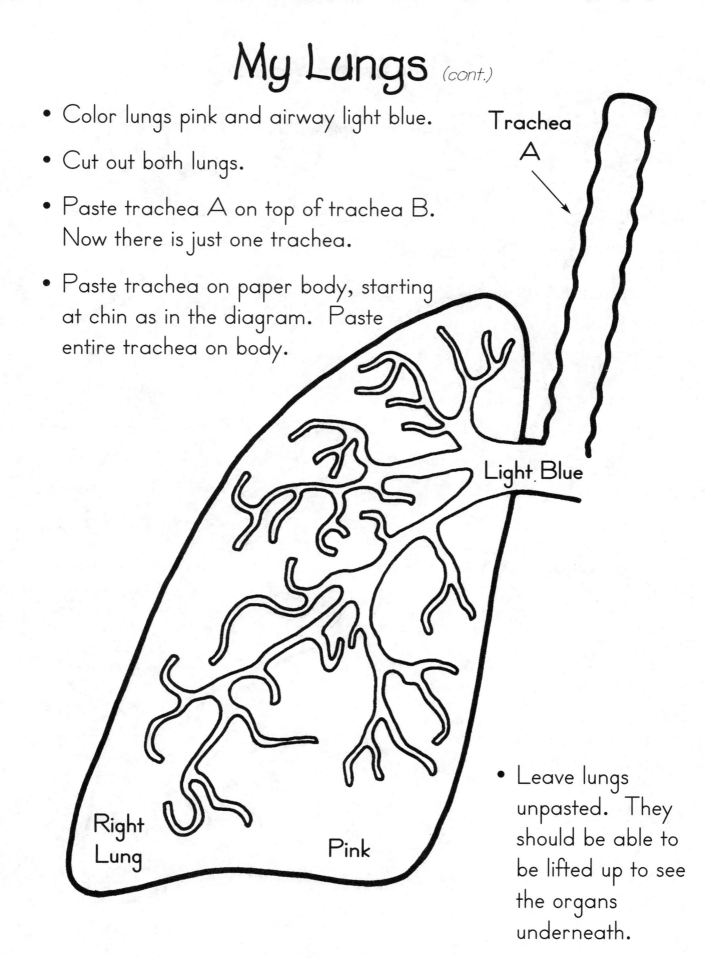

Trachea
A

Light Blue

Right
Lung

Pink

- Leave lungs unpasted. They should be able to be lifted up to see the organs underneath.

My Lungs *(cont.)*

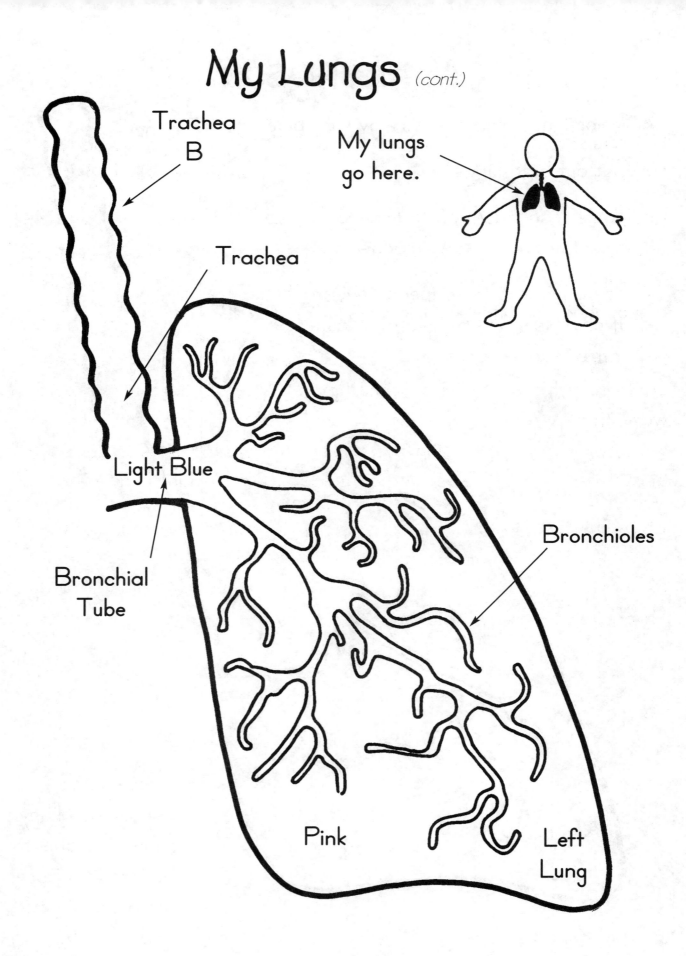

Trachea
B

My lungs
go here.

Trachea

Light Blue

Bronchial
Tube

Bronchioles

Pink

Left
Lung

My Skin

My skin is a very large organ. It covers every inch of my body. When I am an adult, I will have about seven pounds of skin!

My skin is a cover for my body. It is thick and strong. Most of the time my skin keeps my body from getting hurt. If I do get hurt and my skin is cut or scraped, my body can make new skin to take its place. My skin is growing all the time.

If I look closely at my skin, I can see many things. I can see hairs. I can see wrinkles. I can also see tiny holes called pores. My pores let water from inside my body come out. My body gets rid of liquid waste by sweating through my pores. Sweat also helps to keep my body from getting too hot or too cold.

I have many nerve endings in my skin. These nerve endings send messages to my brain. I can feel different things because of these nerve endings. I can feel heat and cold. I can feel pain. And I can feel touch like when I get hugged!

My Eyes

My eyes see for me. They are like little cameras that take a picture and send the picture to my brain. Then, my brain tells me what I have seen. My eyes show me things that look pretty, like a tree, and things that help me learn, like books.

My eyes have tears that help to clean them when they get dirty. My tears also wet my eyes every time I blink. This way, my eyes won't get too dry. Tears in my eyes also show when I am sometimes sad or hurt.

My eyes show me many things.

My Nose

My nose smells for me. It helps me smell the smells I like and the smells I don't like. I can smell flowers and I can smell burnt toast. My nose sends the smells to my brain, and my brain tells me what I have smelled.

My nose also cleans and warms the air I breathe. Inside my nose, I have little hairs to catch dirt and dust. I also have a thick, sticky liquid called mucus that catches the dirt and dust that get past the little hairs. Sometimes the dirt and dust make me sneeze!

My Ears

If I look closely at the word "hear," I can see the word "ear" in it! My ears hear for me. They can hear very loud sounds. They can even hear very, very quiet sounds.

The part of my ear that I can see catches all kinds of sounds. It sends the sounds to the rest of my ear, which is inside my head. My ears change the sounds into nerve messages. These nerve messages are then sent to my brain. My brain tells me what I heard!

My Tongue

My tongue helps me do many things. It helps me chew and swallow. It helps me speak. My tongue also helps me taste.

The top side of my tongue has tiny nerve endings on it. These nerve endings are called taste buds. My taste buds help me taste things that are sweet or salty. They also help me taste things that are sour or bitter.

My nose helps me know what I have tasted, too. If I blindfolded you, put a piece of pear in your mouth and let you smell an apple, you would think you ate an apple!

My Face

- Make eyes, eyebrows, a nose, and a mouth. Color eyes and eyebrows the color that yours are. Color the skin of the face the same color as yours. Don't forget to color your ears, too!

- Cut out face. Attach your face to the paper body, pasting only from the nose to the chin. The top part of your face should cover your brain. (Don't put paste on your brain!)

Don't
paste
here.

Paste
here.

- Draw and color your hair on the paper body.

- It is starting to look like you!

My Body Checklist

I need to try to answer "yes" to all these questions every day!

☐ Yes ☐ No   1. Did I get plenty of sleep so my body could rest?

☐ Yes ☐ No   2. Did I eat the food that was best for my body?

☐ Yes ☐ No   3. Did I exercise to help my muscles, heart, and other body parts work better?

☐ Yes ☐ No   4. Did I drink plenty of water?

☐ Yes ☐ No   5. Did I stand and sit straight so my back won't hurt and my body will work better?

☐ Yes ☐ No   6. Did I exercise my brain by thinking and learning?

☐ Yes ☐ No   7. Did I try to be happy all day so my body won't be sad?

How many yes and no answers?

☐   ☐
Yes   No

My name: _____

Today's date: _____

Resources Available from Teacher Created Resources

235   Thematic Unit: *The Human Body* — Intermediate

270   Thematic Unit: *Five Senses* — Primary

278   Thematic Unit: *Food* — Primary

584   Thematic Unit: *My Body* — Pre K–Grade 1

815   Science/Literature Unit: *The Magic School Bus® Inside the Human Body*

2373 Thematic Unit: *Food and Nutrition* — Pre K–Grade 1